RADICAL HUMAN

GUI JEAN-PAUL CHEVALIER

Illustrated by Jayda Transon

Photography By Andre Leif Kivijarvi, Gui Jean-Paul Chevalier.

Copyright © 2016 Gui Jean-Paul Chevalier
All rights reserved. No Material, written or printed in the publication may be reissued, reproduced, sampled, distributed or transmitted in any form, including but not limited to, photocopying, recording, printing by mechanical or electrical methods, without direct permission from the Author and contingent upon an agreeing publisher, except for the specific use of minimal quotations as apart of critical reviews, reports and authorized noncommercial use permitted by national copy right and intellectual property laws.
ISBN-13: 978-0-692-75660-7

Radical Human: The Anthology

Last and First Definition
By Gui Jean-Paul Chevalier

-A point of spirit, referring to a Person's set of resilient, soft and hard codes, tested and proven dedicated to the breaking down of life constructs, inconducive to the delicate, and secret complexities of our ever-emergent humanity.

Contents

1. All Sides at Lock (7)
2. *Innocence Has Out-lived the Mouth's Tomb (8)*
3. *Selective Light (11)*
4. We are those Who Revive the Chain (13)
5. The Gift of a Stranger (14)
6. Red (16)
7. Neighbor or Stranger (17)
8. Inner Space (18)
9. Flip the Judge (20)
10. I know (21)
11. Hammer and Groove (23)
12. Paths (24)
13. The Star (25)
14. *Territory of Lies* (27)
15. In the Ring of Stars (30)
16. Choke, Repel and Fear (31)
17. For Tomorrow (32)
18. Arabian Desert (33)
19. We Call it Survival (34)
20. Rust (35)
21. In the Tube (37)
22. Stolen (38)
23. There is an Alter at every Pleaded Well (40)
24. The Leaning Tree (41)
25. *The Dummy's Wooden Heart* (43)
26. Boxes like Cubes (45)
27. Clapping with the Wrong Choir (46)

28. Running Contention plays Longer than Paraded Worlds (47)
29. Alpha-Ant (48)
30. High Power (50)
31. Cold Knowledge (51)
32. *The Starving Farmer* (52)
33. When a Name Becomes no More (55)
34. The Sound of Dreams (56)
35. Miles to Gold (57)
36. A Light in the Ghosttown (58)
37. Center (60)
38. *The Absolution Hour* (61)
39. What the Funnel knows (64)
40. *All Seeds at Rest* (65)

All Sides at Lock

The fulcrum of inner justice is
decided
No Departed thought
will persuade the scale

Serenity is content

My faith will not blink to the flash of
light

In the seconds of now,
Between space of mind and cluttered
question
You lost the link to living sight.

Innocence has Out-Lived the Mouth's Tomb

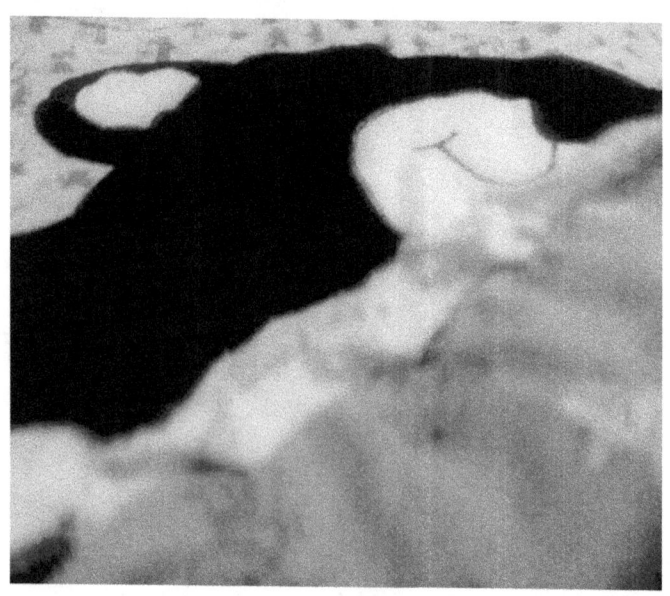

I am the Heart of a child
dressed in old leaves
Behind sparks of light,
and the Red wall of protection
is the soft, invitation;
Blue, Tranquil, like the spirit's eye of the
flame.
A tear in the night mourns as it meets earth,
for chopped roots
A wrinkle for the day, and be it a dozen
for a neighbor's dry sprout

I am the Ray
like forgotten dust
Running, Tripping
over emotion to embrace serenity
at the bedrock of every soul-cord vine

I Plea with Strength

I shield the gems like a nest wrapped in the falls of cedar

Selective Light

Everything is Real
The Idea you want to forget is what will only heal
The notion of none is more than no

Buried out of sight is only deeper in the mind.
The fear of what might exist
in the absence of now,
Can't forgive wishful lines
as they recall what never made a vow

In the light of all anything known,
lies a blank surface of nothing found
But in the shadows surrounding center space focus,
Resides what life never sees around.

We Are those who Revive the Chain

Run from us
There's a huddle for coward thought

Divide the wall between renegades of the mind.

As throngs of suppressed promise shiver in the bunker of order
The tears of wasted labor rain down on smudged dreams.

Jump the Barricade of factored Delusion.
Trample the memory of what stifled Ration deems.

The Gift of a Stranger

Buried feeling prepares as mountain
to the lava.
In the passing of endless moons,
A monstrous display brews deep
within

The Voice of a Thousand men
rumbles from the Hillside
Quiet Night will break
To the Prison of Rock and Cave
I no longer Abide

You stand on the ever-shaking
Confidence of your own faults
Who's plate does sandy sin reside?

In the Crevices of my foundation you fed soot and soil.
Thoughts stuck in the Clay

The Cornerstone of my heart's Tolerance
shifts, like in the Conviction of a sinner

Landslide.
No dream or spirit shall fall like the ashes to come.

Hear the call through the beautiful Evergreens,

Run far and wide. Find Persistence.
Scale the Rugged Range in the safety of a stranger's Distance

Red

We live in Declaration state
Sign the code, Preach the word
Magnify our fate.

Arms of the enemy rise to tear down,
Sync to Destruction
Red flags light Red Lights
Supreme threat sounds the alarm.

The captain of my heart calls the order
Destiny and discernment find ally.
Fail safe.
In unison, forces from the bunker of sacred preservation assemble
Many years, One voice.

Neighbor or Stranger

Sleep
Neighbor the day
Stranger the night
Life

Home is inner. I am mine
Soul in Box
I am safe
Cross no lone
Sacred heart. I cherish my locks

Keys to doors you enter in
Some, I'll never hold

Neighbor or Stranger; You'll never know
My voice whispers yes or no.

Inner Space

I am the son
Born of light eclipsed by the lie of the sun.
No Child of known world
Parent of invisible evidence birthed me.
Brother to rulers of distant fields of matter
At galaxies apart,
speed is to the dead as rain is to the fish
In the shadows of sight, I form to my own,
align to teachings of the inner.
Magnetic pole.

To Creator I am here
To knowledge but a mystery

As seasons change, I crescent like the moon
A new spark to old ways of night
shifts the dust of forgotten life

The worlds around my orbit,
throw lingering eyes like meteors.
As they slowly rotate,
Only to Marvel again.
My gravity calibrates to System Spirit home.
Pods of alike follow tracks of order
I feed from solar rays self-universal
No mind, no one knows me.
I am my own happy planet.

Flip the Judge

In Rags of Goth I laid
Under the brimstone glare,
I offered with the might of a Beggar.

Though Shunned as a Leper,
I'm cleansed by the spirit within.

Filth to the eye of iniquity is foolish;
Ever hidden.

I Know

Born of a spark
Forged in the flame like purified gold

I became

From the dust
I absorb no conventional nutrient

Like the evergreens I synthesize
poison

Reveal

As I rise I breath resilience
My eyes see intuition

The focus of my core

Reads fierce

I'm protected by the spanning
distance of long learned heart.
Nothing Shall Pierce

Hammer and Groove

Dance the cloud of a sinners mind.
Are you caught in the groove.
Hold the wall of safety to avoid the fall of the deep
Anchored to the right of concrete,
Ask do I feel free
To the unrestricted, and to the rooted rod
A magnetic pulse throbs.

The beat is the life force
Who, is to die first?

Paths

I know where truth lives
In the magic of night air bliss,
You led the way,
effortless like a breath
Within the shadows of the evening's
blind heart
The arrow of fate
At the fork in our spirit's path is
flipped

At the noon day hour
The playground of dreams
Resembles no starry field of paradise
Can't find the landmark to your soul.
The light of suppressed wonder
Reveals Divots in the trail of Gold

The Star

Speeding,
Won't wait for time
In the thick of Galaxy Jungle
Faster than a thief's night

I'm speeding

Ways of rays orbit all around
No given permission
Stuck on a track
Vain mission.
In the light of day
Oblivion mirrors shadows and her
night

We crashed
Through the air so dark

Between bangs of light
I missed the star
I missed the start of magic, vivid,
right.

Territory of Lies

GUI JEAN-PAUL CHEVALIER

Who's Lie is Right
Beside the stone of truth,
Who resides?
Do bombs of empty air from a blind mouth
Speak knowledge
Or is it the blood of weary trodden feet
that lay the path to Justice
Buried lies

the rocks of the road have charred my soles
like the fire's smoking red coals

In the desert, the Mirage paints a delusion:
you see what mirror forgot.

Throw shades of ash on what screams:
I'm real.

The Color of understanding lies
Beneath a coat of Blackened judgement.
Shadow.

What is here,
The abyss of Vacant thought?
Or the scars that forge my zeal.

In the Ring of Stars

I am no Prerogative
I am every priority
Discard no year in perusing the crevices,
My moving mind won't shelve
Take no station.

Genius death is seat to the back
Look within to look ahead
I'm not Middle of your Mind's pack
Meet or mend your thoughts
My sparks are booked
Reservation: Top Slot
Take a date, Beautiful time is spendy Business.

Only stars give it all.

Choke, Repel and Fear

Here,
In secrets of mind
Caught in the smoke of sparked thought,
lives the wind to breath again
Neighbor to forgotten demon

Restless like a Vision
it burns memory on the wick of patience.

Sheltered from the light of view,
Are the coded confines of Collateral Rule.

For Tomorrow

While today rest on Filtered time
Memories of past nights,
sleep off forgotten dreams

Who carried the chains of then?
Did I rust in the Journey

The link of start to now
Fogs in the haze of ungrateful effort
and
focused pause.

Arabian Desert

In the darkness of the night
In the stillness of stagnation
I see a drinking well

Sandy winds blow
Sting my virgin eyes
I'm walking closer to hell
In the dry storm of the desert
I am without
Give me some within
At the well I make known my wish
To the glistening waters of the
Arabian Sea, I give in

I could look away in an instance
Will your echoing call quench my
resistance.

We call it Survival

I've gotten weary,
Years of intrusion
at quarters too close for calm nights
I've curled up like a sick child by the
Winter fire
Incubate

This tired. . .

The hustle of whispering doubt and
the rumpus of ill-minded inquiry
left the soul Parched of sanity's
Reservoir

Will a dose of quietude heal time?
Rid the system for toxin laced
thoughts.

Rust

Where there once was Abundant,
Plentiful, and Merciful
-lies a barren land.

From the hand I gave.

Thousands

I ask.

For the farmer has nourished you
with showers of kindness and sweet
forgiveness
Patience has dried like the roots in
your garden
of bitter fruit and smiling honey do's

My hour is done,
My toiling is over

Seven times over I have churned the soil.

-Fed the flock

Weeds have never known the clock

In the Tube

The cord of light;
A line of un-evading history
Loyal like a sinner.
As it pulls, it flips Memory from
Minuet
Future from False
If to slip, find a coil like all over again
dyslexia

Stretch the line or stretch your mind
What is.
Hear.
Is despair wise or do they just leave it
behind.

Stolen

I walked with a Stolen dream
Across lakes and time you Return

I lost the gem, forgiveness burns,
I'm rocked

Doubt, bliss, and dumb lies run in circuit.

Link.
Stars align in the second of a blink.
Monotonous minuet can't move the moon to see
Holy premonition feels Divine and Dirty
Heaven is adamant as Destiny

In the abyss, serenity hangs sturdy

Maker molds sin, minuet, and magic

I danced with the beautiful, elusive, ghost.

There is an Altar at every Pleaded Well.

Get, off it.

Let diseased thought privatize
beneath itching skin
Blister.

Penetrate the Portal to deeds of your own
Substitute the blood of indefensible rape
for the Sweat of Sober labor

Let it be a washing
Cleans yourself in the tears of guilt
and re-point the compass of prayer to never waver.

The leaning tree

The tide is coming in
The wind is blowing strong
My anchored tree is leaning
Rooted in rock, now foundation
erodes.

Every wave soothes the sore
I'm Leaning.
Momentum coddles Direction
In the storm they hold fast.

Connection.

Water will win
Human nature, are you sin?
My branches behave like sails
When this tree falls

Home they will dig to birth
Those so faithful roots

After the storm
To return back to earth.

The Dummy's wooden Heart

Circus world
I'm in disguise,
Am I whom I seem to be

Revise

From beneath the purple vail
lies glittered perception
Eyes Steer

Is your mind the puppeteer
For what integrity have a mask
Only if thought conceals the synthetic

What is real?
Stupidity Asks.

Boxes like Cubes

As the blocks of time tumble along
monotonous day
The building of beyond
Forgets the memory of then.
Vacant victory
The direction of city path,
-of polished route
Is confused like the maze.

At the turn of every Practiced Corner
The edge, Carves a layer off genius
Mind

Minutes shave.
In Ridged destination,
What good is left
On the grid of Spirit Theft.

Clapping with the Wrong Choir

Break the internal fight.
Discard the voice of over-dated wish

Lest it Teach you the ways of the
Wagon Runner

-Singing hymns to cracked rocks
in the fields of respected existence.

Pray higher than hope

The right of Printed dreams never
begged for her Justice

Running Contention Plays longer than Paraded Worlds

I denounce waters of the Fall.
After pretend pose,
Lined with confused and trusted game of experimental.
For under-shot stars
False rides to subordinate realities,
In battles to lose where pride should never rest.
Through filters of dire heart and the mind's counted Availability,
A foreign fold casts new light on Inviting cliff.

In new sight,
I hold to Reigns of old and Ladders to first Call.

Alpha-Ant

From the barrel of Patriarch cannon
shelves the Chamber of inverted hatred.
It fears what exposes its Rotten core
As it studies from the Library of Lead,
it retains all it has:
Fire
Flame
Fame
Stands tall for all to salute

Every fallen soldier
stamps a badge of honor on a purple ill heart

Pump the Pride

In the Arch of the cylinder
lies a Ring of cold Protection

Fear of self-dissection
Stoic Contemplation

Its aluminum apprehension Sweeps
like a radar,
Scanning for confidence, as it
desecrates the very spirit it needs.

Competence.

High Power

Two sins break the wall
From the seat perched high,
Atop hierarchy's moral stained Altar
Fires the shot of delusion doused force.
Obscure as life to end life
Lofty rank feeds on the width of the barrel.
The Pointed pillar affords Power.
From the altitude nest,
-From the coward-studded, fortified safety of the Tower's bird eye
Lives the haze of gun-smoke's spirit-demon Dyslexia.
Spirit Demon
Demon Spirit.
Battleland of Asphyxiation

Cold Knowledge

What's your Narrative
What's your Cognitive Legacy

What dangles out of spoken view,
-of purposeful effort.

Did the thoughts of now leave a stain
in the mind
Does the Image of intention match
the mirror of impact
What's the weight of Intention.
Does it flow with ease like forgiven
mistake

Or is character as Clumsy as a Whim

The Starving Farmer

With each passing of the moon
What have the hours of nutrients
taught the mind of yesterday's drought.
What has Stagnant Process acquired
from the hands of foiled time.
The gates of invitation swing on rusty hinges

Every Rising Ray of Teaching Light finds a
cloud of Apprehension.

The Ambiguous swirl of season's display,
frightens the Comfort of Countryside
Prediction.

Tend to the fields of ripe Existence

As the Horizon paints the sight of Dry plains

The speed of Mountain Shadow lazily stretches Swifter than the Preparation of your unsifted Understanding

When a Name Becomes no More

I am Gone
I am Better than Dead

The heat of your projected fire
will spark Contemplation as reflected

Feel Every pinch of sin

Dine with the poison of your famous love

Set in the seat of purest hatred

You bought the prayer to stir your soul.

The Sound of Dreams

From out of a dream
Prophecy and fate battle
In the existence of the bursting star
Love Lust Spirit Demon
Bang and rattle
 In the clamor I borrowed a vision
The shine blinds me to see my own sight.
Space and time reflect off the angled moon.
You appear, Rotation and Position placed us near.
I am between the Gravity of Magnetic fields.

Perch my Clouds in the Dreamland of Mirage Lagoon.

Miles to Gold

I want to Reach it
Did I leave prints on the pearly Gates.
When will time end.
Who's year last longer than mine.
Am I mine

How long is fate
Does it quiver longer than the
drought of my outstretched doubt.

A Light in the Ghosttown

In the Ashy Ghosttown of love's battlefield,
I feel a Foreign Friend
In the mirror of the grey and lifeless,
I see what magic will Provoke
Beyond the evening smoke,
a colorful ray of warm light burst through
In the distance, protruding from the rubble, despair breaks.
-A feeling ever new

Life breaths through a Glowing beam
As it nourishes weary thirsty roots,
her illumining aura Pierces home.
Through the soot and bones I am fed
Resurrection is Revolution

I am Alive

My hue radiates in the clouds
and luscious falls of Healing water
soothes the burns
Divine nectar Singes my Pain
The drought has ended
Famine has lost its Reign

Center

In the center of the storm
I am at the center of mind

Buried in the quietude of sacred muse,
ruckus muffles in the distance

Anchored to Foundation
Behind the reach of timed faith,

My heart Meditates with the Spirit of nature

The Absolution Hour

A Ray of Redemption
shines from just beyond the Mountainside
hills

The peak of forgiveness sets fast like the sun.

I have toiled across every distant land
Around the rotation of the world
No victory run.

The window of prayer is closing
Red sky is line of sight.

Bow to the west of Pride
before the howl of night sets in.

The hand of the clock yields no more than fate
The day is done

Your time has come

For soon, behind miles of Rocky time,
Like memories of dust,
I will forever hide.

What the funnel knows

In the space of now, the breath of memory
lives in the Reservoirs of Tomorrow.
In this stolen stretch of shadowed thought,
The projection of ticking existence awakens to the Prophecy of secret Horizon.

Promise is sound

Let withered efforts of time
find the dawn.
For the storms of yesterday's folly
never swirl forgotten in vain.

All Seeds at Rest

As the roots of existence dangle out of crumpled dirt
I call upon the Physician of the Pasture

Leaves tumble in the distance

The rows of years lay stretched wide,
longing for that fruitful harvest
My stalk stands at the middle
of nothing and nothing
from the wind

But in the soil between stifled sprout
and my neighbors vine
Yields the potion to nourish every fiber than may bend

The Pungent, sweet Blossoming herbs of
Ancient day
to soothe the soul
rid the virus
Lie nestled in a golden patch of Lily dreams
at Rhododendron Garden

About The Author:Gui Jean-Paul Chevalier was born in the United States, in the city of Renton, Washington, in January, 1990. Though born in the state's most populated county, he calls most memories home to his childhood residence on a 24-acre farm in Washington's rural Whatcom County, just south of British Columbia, Canada. The second born of three, son to a then homeschool teacher and stay at home mother, and a late-hour refinery worker, he spent his summer afternoons on the bike, racing around the property with his first brother Laurent, and to this day, spends his Sunday mornings at the pew. Though the artist mind was always there, It wasn't until his High School years that more creative outlets became available. He joined the Mariner High School Chamber choir at 17, and competed to win the Bronze award in 2007 at annual Fullerton College competition in Fullerton California.

At the fall of 2008, he would enroll at Northwest University in Kirkland, Washington, where he would join the Northwest University Eagle Debate team. Winning awards for competitive academic rigor, consecutively from 2010-2012, he quickly found a new love and appreciation for rhetoric and writing. After graduating with a Bachelors of art degree in Organizational Communication, he would start his career as an Assistant Debate Coach.

It was his love for debate, songwriting, and his involvement in activism that would be the three most striking endeavors of his life.
At the close of 2014, he would begin his participation in social activism, around issues of homelessness and racial injustice. In 2015 he would write his first newspaper article for the award-winning Seattle publication, Real Change.

The Radical Human Decloration:
I Will Be Celebrated for the Space I occupy

Notes in Reflective Review

I write this Because Life is real. Because the added of wrongs can find new absences if we decide to hold strong on, to our best humanity. I write this because life is visceral, and because all we have is each other. If to live
The only un-bought chance as this, we ought to live and be supported for all we are, not all wished to cram, conform. Let mysteries speak to the beautiful abyss they are. In instances of trouble, or in times of difficulty, hear me, let my cries fall on receptive, guilt-reluctant, un-feared ears. Hear with the ears of granting delight, presumptive good thought and replace slots of misused memory with the knowledge of heart over-due; now knowns. The Radical Human, holds with inner strength all the cords that bundle the sacred gems and form the only I, we can know, independent of claws to strip edits of my unsuspecting soul.
This I Vow.

www.ingramcontent.com/pod-product-compliance
Lightning Source LLC
Chambersburg PA
CBHW071240090426
42736CB00014B/3162